ACADIA'S
Native Flowers, Fruits, and Wildlife

A C A D I A ' S
Native Flowers, Fruits, and Wildlife

Text and photographs by Steve Perrin

Flowers and fruits presented in the order of their seasonal appearance

Eastern National

ACADIA'S
Native Flowers, Fruits, and Wildlife

Copyright © 2001 by Stephen G. Perrin
Printed in the United States of America
ISBN 1-888213-80-9

Front cover
White-tailed deer fawn

Inside front cover
Fireweed, *Epilobium angustifolium*, July—August

Back cover
Witherod, *Viburnum nudum,* berries turning pink to blue, August

Inside back cover
Rattlesnake plantain leaves

Frontispiece
Big-leaved Aster, *Aster macrophyllus*, August

Title page
Beaver lodges, Breakneck Road pond

Contents page
White-tailed deer fawn

Published by
Eastern National
470 Maryland Drive
Fort Washington, PA 19034
www.eParks.com

CONTENTS

PREFACE

Acadia National Park is one of the most popular recreational destinations in New England. What is it that three million people a year come here to see and to do? Certainly they hope to enjoy the park's famous coastal hills, ponds, shores, scenic drives, carriage roads, and hiking trails.

Too, they come to take part in the life of Acadia, for Acadia is alive, teeming with native plants and wildlife thriving in local habitats under conditions that prevail year after year.

From April through October, Acadia's living landscape varies week to week. Leaf buds open, flower buds turn to blossoms that, pollinated, turn to berries, inviting wildlife to feed. Then leaves turn from green to orange and red, they fall, and bare branches wave above snow crisscrossed with tracks.

Personal discovery of such plant and animal life enriches everyone's visit to Acadia. These pages highlight many of the species along the park's roads and trails that can be spotted in their native haunts. Flowers and fruits are arranged not by color or family but in the order of their seasonal appearance.

Every week—every day—Acadia is different. What is out there waiting to be discovered? Today is a good day to find out.

THANKS

Neither botanist nor biologist, the author is grateful for help and suggestions offered by:

Deb Wade, Chief Interpreter, Acadia National Park

Linda Gregory, Botanist, Acadia National Park

Bruce Connery, Wildlife Biologist, Acadia National Park

Wanda Moran, Information Park Ranger, Acadia National Park

Kristen Britain, Writer/Editor, Acadia National Park

Craig Greene, Newlin Professor of Botany, College of the Atlantic

Barbara Cole and Susan Leiter, co-chairs, Wild Gardens of Acadia

Thomas F. Vining, co-author of *Flora of Maine*

Constance S. Stubbs, Biological Sciences Department,
University of Maine, Orono

Richard G. Dearborn, Survey Entomologist,
Insect and Disease Laboratory, Maine Forest Service

Ellsworth Photo Center:
Yvonne Andrews, Amy Ely, Eric Perkins, Mary Turner

Dale Swensson, designer, Swensson Design and Associates

Dan Burk, Penmor Lithographers

Jason Scarpello, Publications Manager, Eastern National

Taxonomy follows Haines and Vining,
Flora of Maine (Bar Harbor: V. F. Thomas Co., 1998)

INTRODUCTION

The challenge facing every national park is to promote visitors' enjoyment of its outstanding features without putting those same features at risk from careless, inappropriate, or excessive use. Acadia's network of motor roads, carriage roads, and hiking trails does a superb job of taking visitors to see nature in action while, at the same time, protecting that action from abuse.

As guests of the park, it is up to us to avoid trampling plants underfoot, to admire flowers without picking them, to enjoy chance encounters with wildlife without baiting it with snacks.

Acadia is alive at every step because of the integrity of its natural habitats. The plants that thrive here do so because this is their kind of place. The soil is right, rainfall is right, temperature is right, sunlight is right, companion species are right, and freedom from interference is right. The same is true for Acadia's wildlife. This is their homeland, the land that makes them what they are. Native plants and animals are vivid expressions of the local climate and terrain. They are Acadia's watersheds come to life.

Most park visitors live in localities that have been altered to favor human activities. Acadia is a place where such development is kept to a minimum. *Vive la difference!* That is what draws us here. We come to connect with life in its native state. We are born to seek out lichens, mosses, ferns, trees, flowers, berries, and wildlife. We have survived in their company for millions of years. They are our neighbors; without them we wouldn't be here.

Acadia is a living display of our better half: it is a window on the support system that provides us with healthy soils, pure water, clean air, sunlight, plants, animals—the necessities of life.

It is no accident we seek out scenic surroundings. The experience of beauty is our personal response to vigor and health. Natural beauty is a sure sign we are where we belong. It tells us we would do well to stick around. We are made to appreciate our earthly companions—flowers in bloom, clusters of berries, insects and birds on the wing, signs of secret life in the woods. This is our habitat, too, or used to be. It awakens us to our former selves who were once native to earlier Acadias much like this.

HOW ACADIA WORKS

Acadia is powered by sunlight and gravity under the influence of a climate featuring an average of 50 inches of precipitation a year, temperatures ranging between 90°F. and minus 10°F., and winds blowing from the southwest in summer, northwest in winter. Precipitation peaks in November and December with about 6 inches a month, gradually declines through August to a low of some 3 inches, then increases in the fall.

Almost 100 small watersheds on Mount Desert Island direct the flow of water downward across slopes into low areas and valleys, storing moisture in the soil, releasing it slowly, providing a reliable supply of water and nutrients to the roots of plants through the growing season between April and October.

Plants use water, air, and sunlight to carry on their business of food production, growth, repair, defense, and reproduction. Given a temperate climate moderated by the Gulf of Maine, Acadia's soils and terrain govern the local availability of sunlight and water, setting conditions favoring one plant over another. The survivors attract compatible species of wildlife that nest among them, pollinate their flowers, and by eating their fruit, spread their seeds.

Summits tend to be hot and dry with scant soil, valleys to be cool and wet with thicker soil. Slopes feature moderate conditions that vary between the two extremes. Some plants (pickerelweed, hobblebush) like wet roots, so are common in Acadia's lowland areas. Others (mountain sandwort, bearberry) thrive in direct sunlight on dry ridges and summits. A great many plants are moderate in their tastes (beech, white pine) and make their home between lowlands and summits. Still other plants tolerate a range of conditions (blueberry, meadowsweet) and thrive throughout the park.

The carriage and motor roads connecting Jordan Pond and Eagle Lake follow the valley shared by those waters. The Jesup and Kane trails are valley trails, as are the Hunters Brook, Gorge, Giant Slide, Valley, Valley Cove, and Great Pond trails, among others. Such routes lead through habitats where valley plants live.

Acadia is famous for the ridge trails running along the spines of many of its prominent peaks, good places to spot pitch pines, black chokeberry, three-toothed cinquefoil, mountain sandwort, and orange grass. The park also has its share of trails scaling cliffs from valley floors to summits, including the Precipice, Notch, Cadillac Mountain West Face, Canon Brook, and Bubbles-Pemetic trails. The Newport and Jordan Cliffs trails traverse steep, rocky slopes bearing a surprising variety of flowering plants.

FLOWERS

From our school days, we remember something about pistils and stamens. Flowers, we recall, have parts, and those parts play an important role in plant reproduction.

The parts of simple flowers are specialized leaves arranged in whorls around a common center. The innermost whorl is the female part of a flower. It contains one or more pistils lifting stigmas on thin stalks above an ovary. When a grain of pollen attaches to a stigma, it germinates, sending sperm through a pollen tube to fertilize an egg, a future seed.

The male part, a whorl of pollen-producing stamens, surrounds the female part. An attractive and often colorful array of petals embraces both pistils and stamens, serving to draw the attention of pollinating insects or birds. In many flowers the petals are joined to form a bell, funnel, or tube. A protective whorl of sepals forms an outer covering that, opening or blooming, exposes the inner whorls when conditions are right and pollinators are apt to be near.

Many flowers seem more complex than such a simple plan suggests, but in their own ways they express variations on that basic arrangement. Flower parts can be displayed radially about a center, or symmetrically across a vertical midline.

A few plant species assure genetic diversity by separating the sexes. They have two kinds of flowers, male and female. The different sexes may be on the same plant (birches) or on different plants (staghorn sumac). To avoid self-pollination, some flowers (fireweed) feature stamens and pistils at different stages as they bloom.

Many plants reproduce without flowers. Mosses use surface water such as dew to convey sperm from male to female plants. Cone-bearing trees such as spruces and pines rely on the wind to carry pollen from male to female cones. But reliance on fertilization by wind and water is a hit-or-miss affair. It works best in small localities where conditions are relatively stable year after year.

Flowering plants are a recent success story about 125 million years old. Conifers have been around for some 270 million, mosses for 360 million, ferns for 400 million years. Flowering plants that rely on the wind to transport their pollen (grasses, nettles) put scant energy into colorful displays or attractive scents; their flowers are greenish, inconspicuous, and odorless.

Animals have co-evolved with flowering plants. Humans are no exception. Our food supply depends on fewer than twenty species which we harvest or cultivate.

Plants that rely on wildlife pollinators have gained a survival edge by attracting the notice of mobile insects, birds, or other animals.

Flowers offer such wanderers food in exchange for help in transferring pollen from one plant to another. Adult bees feed on floral nectar, and use pollen to feed their young. They locate appropriate flowers by scent, then rely on color, shape, and texture in approaching individual blossoms. Dusted with pollen from other—often distant—flowers, a bee will brush some of those grains onto the stigma of each flower it visits.

Moths and butterflies are also prominent pollinators. Drawn by scents and pale colors, many insects approach flowers at night to escape the vigilant eyes of their predators. Certain odorless flowers (cardinalflower, columbine, wood lily) are pollinated by ruby-throated hummingbirds drawn to their striking red color.

Not all of Acadia's flowers are native to the habitats where they now grow. Many introduced flowers have escaped from cultivation (golden-chain tree, lupine), or are immigrants inadvertently carried by human traffic from other regions (hawkweed, rugosa rose). This book features a selection of flowering plants that are native to Mount Desert Island.

An excellent way to find out what native plants are currently blooming in the park is to visit the Wild Gardens of Acadia at Sieur de Monts Spring. Maintained by the Bar Harbor Garden Club, the gardens contain specimens of over 400 native plants growing in twelve different habitat areas.

FRUITS

Plant hormones in grains of pollen prompt flower ovaries to grow into seed-bearing fruit. Once underway, fruiting is driven by hormones produced by the ovary itself. The end result is a fruit where a fertilized flower was before.

Fruits come in many different types. *Berries* contain seeds embedded in pulpy flesh. *Drupes* (pin cherry) have a single hard stone. *Hips* enclose rose seeds in a tough, protective case. *Pomes* (hawthorn) enclose seeds in a thin, fibrous membrane around the core. *Aggregates* (raspberry) are clumps of attached berries. *Accessories* (strawberry) display hard seeds around fleshy interiors.

Many berries are eaten by wildlife and spread in their feces. Blueberry seeds will not grow unless they pass through an animal's digestive tract. In July and August, flocks of gulls settle on Acadia's mountain ledges to gorge on ripe blueberries, doing themselves and the berries a favor.

Several low evergreen plants (partridgeberry, mountain cranberry, wintergreen) display bright red berries through the winter. Sumac berries containing tannic acid are not the first to be eaten, but after being rinsed by rain and melting snow, the spires of red fruit provide a much needed meal to crows, thrushes, and deer, among others. A few berries (bluebead, baneberry) are known or suspected to be poisonous to humans.

WILDLIFE

Acadia hosts over 273 species of birds. Many are year-round residents, including loons, guillemots, eiders, herring gulls, black ducks, eagles, owls, crows, blue jays, woodpeckers, chickadees, nuthatches. A great many others are summer residents (peregrine falcons, ospreys, turkey vultures, thrushes, warblers, sparrows). Winter residents include many species that breed in Northern Canada (grebes, oldsquaws, harlequin ducks, buffleheads, goldeneyes). Migrants heading south pass through in late summer and early fall (shorebirds, hawks, warblers).

For some visitors, wildlife means primarily mammals. Acadia has its share, but most are wary of people as potential predators. Chipmunks and both red and gray squirrels are common, as are other rodents such as muskrats, beavers, porcupines, meadow voles, and various mice. Acadia's weasels include mink, ermine, long-tailed weasel, striped skunk, and river otter. Early rising visitors are apt to meet white-tailed deer anywhere in the park. Snowshoe hares are common but secretive, as are red fox and eastern coyote.

As a note of caution, rabies has recently been found on Mount Desert Island; no animal should be approached or offered food.

Acadia is home to several species of salamanders, frogs, turtles, and snakes, none of them venomous. Snakes are often seen disappearing into trailside underbrush. The most common is the garter snake, but ringneck, red-bellied, smooth green, and Northern milk snakes are at home here as well. Frogs are more often heard than seen, including pickerel frogs, bullfrogs, green frogs, wood frogs, and spring peepers.

Along saltwater shores, barnacles, mussels, clams, and crabs are common species of shellfish. Seals, porpoises, and great whales (minke, finback, humpback) frequent the park's offshore waters. Many of Acadia's ponds have been dammed since early settlement days; in some cases, their native fish species are maintained or supplemented by the state's stocking program. Free-flowing streams support populations of brook trout, American eel, and more than a dozen nongame fish.

As you explore Acadia, you are bound to meet spiders and insects, or signs of them at least: springtails in winter; blackflies, bumblebees, and mourning cloaks in spring; water striders, butterflies, moths, dragonflies, ants, and countless others all summer long, and a lingering few in the fall. Foggy mornings reveal the artistry of web-weaving spiders in intricate bowl-and-doily, orb, funnel, and sheet-web designs.

Wildlife signs are encountered more often than wildlife on the hoof or wing. Wherever you go you are apt to come across nests, beaver lodges, eggshells, feathers, scats, nipped twigs, tufts of hair, and tracks in sand, mud, or snow.

FLOWERS

Spring, summer, and fall, **non-native flowers** (such as lupine, hawkweed, orange hawkweed, daisy) thrive in the disturbed soils along Acadia's roads and carriage roads.

Mayflower

(trailing-arbutus)
Heath Family
Epigaea repens
Where: sandy woods
When: *April – May*

Hobblebush

(witch hobble), Honeysuckle Family, *Viburnum lantanoides*
Where: moist woods   When: **May**   Fruit, *see page 100*

Bearberry

Heath Family
*Arctostaphylos
  uva-ursi*
Where: open, sandy
  soil; ledges
When: *May*
Fruit, *see page 97*

Pin cherry

(fire cherry, bird cherry), Rose Family, *Prunus pensylvanica*
Where: woods, clearings   When: **May**   Fruit, *see page 93*

Shadbush

(shad, Juneberry, serviceberry), Rose Family, genus *Amelanchier*
Where: woods, clearings   When: *May–June*

Painted trillium

Lily Family, *Trillium undulatum*
Where: moist woods, stream banks   When: **May**   Fruit, *see page 102*

Low, sweet blueberry

Heath Family
*Vaccinium
  angustifolium*
Where: barrens,
  ledges
When: *May–June*
Fruit, *see page 87*

Violet

Violet Family
Viola species
Where: woods,
  meadows
When: *May-June*

Striped maple

(moosewood)
Maple Family
Acer pensylvanicum
Where: understory of
mixed woods
When: *May–June*

Wild sarsaparilla
Gingseng Family
Aralia nudicaulis
Where: woods
When: *May–June*
Fruit, *see page 89*

Wild strawberry

Rose Family, *Fragaria virginiana*
Where: fields, open areas   When: *May–June*

Rhodora

Heath Family, *Rhododendron canadense*
Where: moist thickets, bogs   When: ***May–June***   Fruit, *see page 104*

Black chokeberry

Rose Family, *Photinia melanocarpa*
Where: wet woods, thickets, rock crevices   When: **May – June** Fruit, *see page 107*

Blue-eyed grass

Iris Family
Sisyrinchium
  montanum
  var. *crebrum*
Where: meadows,
  shores, open areas
When: *May – June*

Bunchberry

(dwarf cornel), Dogwood Family, *Cornus canadensis*
Where: moist woods and thickets   When: ***May–June***   Fruit, *see page 96*

Left:
Canada mayflower
(wild lily-of-the-
valley)
Lily Family
*Maianthemum
canadense*
Where: woods
When: *May–June*
Fruit, *see page 118*

Right:
Starflower
Primrose Family
Trientalis borealis
Where: woods, bogs
When: *May–June*

White lady's slipper

A variant pink
   lady's slipper
(moccasin flower)
Orchid Family
Cypripedium acaule
Where: dry woods,
   open areas
When: *May–June*

Pink lady's slipper
(moccasin flower)
Orchid Family
Cypripedium acaule
Where: dry woods,
open areas
When: *May-June*

Golden heather

Rockrose Family, *Hudsonia ericoides*
Where: ledges   When: *May – June*

Jack in the pulpit

Arum Family
Arisaema triphyllum
Where: *moist or wet woods*
When: **May-June**
Fruit, *see page 108*

Cotton grass

Sedge Family
*Eriophorum
    angustifolium*
Where: wetlands
When: *May–July*

Pale corydalis

(tall corydalis)
Poppy Family
Corydalis sempervirens
Where: rocky woods,
 cliffs, talus
When: *May – August*

Black huckleberry

Heath Family, *Gaylussacia baccata*
Where: woods, ledges   When: **June**   Fruit, *see page 98*

Mountain cranberry

(lingonberry), Heath Family, *Vaccinium vitis-idaea* ssp. *minus*
Where: rocky areas, bogs   When: **June**   Fruit, *see page 88*

Labrador tea

Heath Family
*Rhododendron
    groenlandicum*
Where: bogs, rocky
    slopes
When: *June*

Pitcher plant

Pitcher Plant Family, *Sarracenia purpurea*
Where: bogs   When: *June–July*   Leaf, *see page 38*

Pitcher plant leaf

Pitcher Plant Family, *Sarracenia purpurea*
Where: Bogs   When: **year–round**   Flower, *see page 37*

Bluebead-lily

(corn lily, clintonia)
Lily Family
Clintonia borealis
Where: woods
When: *June–July*
Fruit, *see page 90*

Beach-pea

Pea Family
Lathyrus japonicus
Where: gravelly
  shores
When: *June–July*

Arethusa
(swamp-pink,
  dragon's mouth)
Orchid Family
Arethusa bulbosa
Where: bogs
When: *June–July*

Northern blue flag

(blueflag iris)
Iris Family
Iris versicolor
Where: marshes,
  swamps, meadows,
  shores, ditches
When: *June–July*

Three-toothed cinquefoil

(wine-leaf cinquefoil), Rose Family, *Sibbaldiopsis tridentata*
Where: rocky or gravelly soil   When: *June–July*

Stonecrop flower buds

(roseroot), Sedum Family, *Rhodiola rosea*
Where: coastal ledges and cliffs   When: *June–July*

Twinflower

Honeysuckle Family
Linnaea borealis
Where: cool woods,
  cold bogs
When: *June–July*

Indian cucumber root

Lily Family, *Medeola virginiana*
Where: rich woods   When: **June-July**   Fruit, *see page 103*

Bush honeysuckle

Honeysuckle Family
Diervilla lonicera
Where: dry woods,
 rocky places
When: *June–July*

Common wood-sorrel

(northern wood-sorrel), Wood-Sorrel Family, *Oxalis montana*
Where: rich, moist woods   When: *June–July*

Sheep laurel
(lambkill)
Heath Family
Kalmia angustifolia
Where: woods, open
  areas
When: *June–July*

Old-field cinquefoil

(common cinquefoil)
Rose Family
Potentilla simplex
Where: woods, fields,
  thickets
When: *June–July*

Winterberry

(black alder)
Holly Family
Ilex verticillata
Where: wet woods,
  swamps, thickets
When: ***June–July***
Fruit, *see page 114*

Spreading dogbane

Dogbane Family
Apocynum androsaemifolium
Where: fields, roadsides
When: *June–July*

Shinleaf

Pyrola Family
Pyrola elliptica
Where: woods
When: *June–July*

Partridgeberry

Madder Family, *Mitchella repens*
Where: woods   When: ***June–July*** Fruit, *see page 112*

Yellow rattle

Figwort Family, *Rhinanthus minor*
Where: thickets, old fields, roadsides   When: *June–July*

Yellow water-lily

(cow lily, spatterdock, yellow pond lily), Water Lily Family, *Nuphar variegata*
Where: shallow fresh water   When: *June–August*

Mountain sandwort

Pink Family, *Minuartia groenlandica*
Where: exposed, gravelly areas; summits   When: *June–September*

Grass pink

Orchid Family
Calopogon tuberosus
Where: bogs
When: *July*

Whorled loosestrife

Primrose Family
Lysimachia quadrifolia
Where: open woods
When: *July–August*

Swamp candles

(yellow loosestrife,
  swamp loosestrife)
Primrose Family
Lysimachia terrestris
Where: swamps,
  low areas
When: *July–August*

Meadowsweet

Rose Family
Spiraea alba
 var. *latifolia*
Where: fields, open
 areas
When: *July–August*

Orange grass

(pineweed)
St. Johnswort Family
*Hypericum
  gentianoides*
Where: sandy or rocky
  soil, summits
When: *July–August*

Wintergreen

(teaberry, checkerberry), Heath Family, *Gaultheria procumbens*
Where: woods   When: *July–August*   Fruit, *see page 116*

Cowwheat

Figwort Family, *Melampyrum lineare*
Where: woods, bogs, rocky barrens   When: ***July–August***

Wood lily
(wild orange-red lily)
Lily Family
Lilium
  philadelphicum
Where: barrens,
  open woods
When: *July–August*

Large purple-fringed orchid

Orchid Family, *Platanthera grandiflora*
Where: meadows, wet thickets, rich woods   When: *July–August*

Pond-lily
(fragrant water-lily)
Water-Lily Family
Nymphaea odorata
Where: ponds
When: *July–August*

Seaside lungwort

(oysterleaf, seaside
  bluebell)
Borage Family
Mertensia maritima
Where: rocks,
  gravelly sea beaches
When: *July–August*

Common evening primrose

[visited by rosy maple moth]
Evening Primrose Family
Oenothera biennis
Where: fields, roadsides
When: *July-August*

Seaside goldenrod

Goldenrod Family, *Solidago sempervirens*
Where: coastal shores and marshes   When: *July–August*

Rand's goldenrod

Goldenrod Family
Solidago simplex
  var. *randii*
Where: dry ledges,
  rocky banks
When: *July–August*

Common arrowhead

Water Plantain
 Family
Sagittaria latifolia
Where: swamps,
 ponds, streams
When: *July–August*
Fruit, *see page 109*

Pickerelweed

Pickerelweed Family
Pontederia cordata
Where: shallow
  water, marshes
When: *July–August*

Hardhack

(steeplebush)
Rose Family
Spiraea tomentosa
Where: fields, wet
   meadows
When: ***July-August***

Jewelweed

(orange touch-me-not), Touch-Me-Not Family, *Impatiens capensis*
Where: moist woods, wet areas   When: *July–August*

Indian pipe

Pyrola Family
Monotropa uniflora
Where: rich woods
When: *July–August*

Harebell

(bluebell), Bluebell Family, *Campanula rotundifolia*
Where: cliffs, woods, meadows, shores   When: *July–September*

Herb Robert

Geranium Family, *Geranium robertianum*
Where: rocky woods and trails, gravelly shores   When: *July – October*

Sea lavender

(marsh rosemary), Leadwort Family, *Limonium carolinianum*
Where: coastal shores   When: *August*

Pinesap

(false beechdrops)
Pyrola Family
Monotropa hypopithys
Where: woods
When: *August*

Downy rattlesnake plantain

Orchid Family
Goodyera pubescens
Where: sloping woods
When: *August*
Leaf, *see inside back cover*

81

Gall of the earth

Composite Family
*Prenanthes trifoliolata
(Cass.) Fern.*
Where: dry, sandy
  clearings; thickets;
  woods
When: *August–
  September*

Shrubby-cinquefoil

Rose Family
*Pentaphylloides
  floribunda*
Where: meadows,
  ledges
When: *August–
  September*

Pearly everlasting

Composite Family
*Anaphalis
    margaritacea*
Where: dry woods,
    open areas
When: *August–
    September*

Small-flowered agalinis

(purple gerardia)
Broomrape Family
Agalinis paupercula
Where: damp shores
When: *August–*
September

Witch hazel

Witch Hazel Family, *Hamamelis virginiana*
Where: woods   When: *September – October*

FRUITS

Low, sweet blueberry
Heath Family
*Vaccinium
 angustifolium*
Where: barrens,
 ledges
When: fruits in ***July***
Flower, *see page 18*

Mountain cranberry

(lingonberry)
Heath Family
Vaccinium vitis-idaea
  ssp. *minus*
Where: rocky areas,
  bogs
When: fruits in *July*
Flower, *see page 35*

Wild sarsaparilla
["sasparilla"]
Gingseng Family
Aralia nudicaulis
Where: woods
When: fruits in *July*
Flower, *see page 21*

Bluebead-lily

(bluebead, corn lily,
  clintonia)
Lily Family
Clintonia borealis
Where: woods
When: fruits in **July**
Poisonous
Flower, *see page 39*

Bog rosemary

Heath Family, *Andromeda polifolia* var. *glaucophylla*
Where: bogs   When: fruits in *July*

Lesser bur reed

(Eastern bur reed)
Bur Reed Family
*Sparganium
    americanum*
Where: shallow water,
    muddy shores
When: fruits in *July*

Pin cherry
(fire cherry, bird
  cherry)
Rose Family
*Prunus
  pensylvanicum*
Where: woods,
  clearings
When: fruits in *July*
Flower, *see page 15*

Mountain holly

Holly Family, *Nemopanthus mucronatus*
Where: damp woods, thickets, swamps   When: fruits in *August*

Staghorn sumac

Cashew Family
Rhus hirta
Where: open areas,
  roadsides
When: fruits in
  August

Bunchberry

Dogwood Family, *Cornus canadensis*
Where: moist woods and thickets   When: fruits in **August**   Flower, *see page 26*

Bearberry

Heath Family, *Arctostaphylos uva-ursi*
Where: open, sandy soil; ledges   When: fruits in **August**   Flower, *see page 14*

Black huckleberry

Heath Family
Gaylussacia baccata
Where: woods, ledges
When: fruits in
 August
Flower, *see page 34*

Choke cherry

Rose Family, *Prunus virginiana*
Where: thickets, borders, roadsides   When: fruits in *August*

Hobblebush

(witch hobble)
Viburnum Family
*Viburnum
  lantanoides*
Where: moist woods
When: fruits in
  August
(berries turn from
  red to black)
Flower, *see page 13*

American mountain ash

Rose Family, *Sorbus americana*
Where: damp woods   When: fruits in *August*

Painted trillium

Trillium Family
Trillium undulatum
Where: moist woods,
  stream banks
When: Fruits in
  August
Flower, *see page 17*

Indian cucumber root

Lily Family, *Medeola virginiana*
Where: rich woods   When: fruits in **August**   Flower, *see page 46*

Rhodora

Rhododendron Family
*Rhododendron
    canadense*
Where: bogs, moist
    thickets
When: fruits in
    August
Flower, *see page 23*

Large cranberry

(American cranberry), Heath Family, *Vaccinium macrocarpon*
Where: wet, low areas; bogs   When: Fruits in *August*

Solomon's seal

Lily Family, *Polygonatum pubescens*
Where: moist, rocky woods; thickets   When: fruits in *August*

Black chokeberry

Rose Family
Photinia melanocarpa
Where: wet woods,
  thickets, crevices
When: fruits in
  August
Flower, *see page 24*

Jack in the pulpit

(Indian turnip)
Arum Family
Arisaema triphyllum
Where: moist or wet
  woods
When: fruits in
  August
Flower, *see page 31*

Common arrowhead

Water Plantain Family, *Sagittaria latifolia*
Where: swamps, ponds, streams   When: fruits in **August**   Flower, *see page 72*

Red baneberry

(snakeberry), Buttercup Family, *Actaea rubra*
Where: rich woods   When: fruits in **August**   *poisonous*

White baneberry

(doll's eyes), Buttercup Family, *Actaea pachypoda*
Where: rich woods   When: fruits in **August**   *poisonous*

Partridgeberry

Madder Family, *Mitchella repens*
Where: woods   When: fruits in **September**   Flower, *see page 54*

Hawthorn

Rose Family, *Crataegus* species
Where: thickets, open woods, fields   When: fruits in ***September***

Winterberry

(black alder)
Holly Family
Ilex verticillata
Where: swamps, wet
  woods, thickets
When: fruits in
  September
Flower, *see page 51*

Maple-leaved viburnum

(dockmackie)
Viburnum Family
Viburnum acerifolium
Where: rocky woods
When: fruits in
  September

Wintergreen

(teaberry,
  checkerberry)
Heath Family
Gaultheria procumbens
Where: woods
When: fruits in
  September
Flower, *see page 63*

Round-leaved dogwood

Dogwood Family
Cornus rugosa
Where: woods, slopes
When: fruits in
September

Canada mayflower
(wild lily-of-the-valley)
Lily Family
*Maianthemum
canadense*
Where: woods
When: fruits in
September
Flower, *see page 27*

WILDLIFE

North America has 450 species of dragonflies, insect predators that can fly forward and backward. Here a colorful **dragonfly** briefly rests at the edge of a wetland.

A striking **dragonfly** with green, compound eyes rests on a spruce branch after devouring a damselfly near Long Pond. Dragonflies are a major control on the park's mosquito population.

A member of the giant silkworm moths, a **luna moth**, *Actias luna*, can measure four-and-a-half inches wingtip-to-wingtip. This one, drawn by a light, landed on the steps of the Rangers Office at park headquarters in early June.

An **Eastern tiger swallowtail**, *Papilio glaucus*, feeds on lilac nectar at the park's Carroll Homestead in Southwest Harbor. This butterfly species visits Acadia's flowers throughout the summer.

Water striders or "skaters" eat mosquito larvae that rise to the surface of Acadia's ponds and small streams. A **common water strider**, *Gerris remigis*, and its reflection press six dimples into the surface of a still pool in the watershed of Eagle Lake.

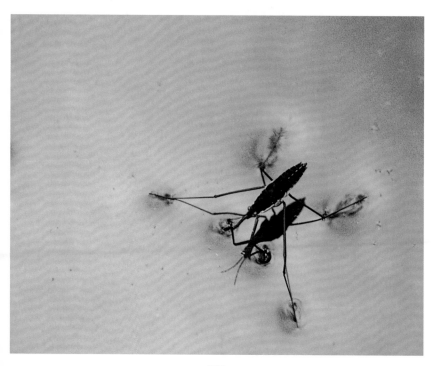

Common aerial yellowjackets, *Dolichovespula arenaria,* build their nests from chewed wood pulp and saliva. This example of insect architecture is suspended from the branch of a maple tree at the south end of Long Pond.

Web-weaving spiders are also accomplished architects. This web in a red spruce sapling was built by a **bowl-and-doily spider**. The rigging snares flying insects while the lower deck protects the spider against attack from the rear.

Black-and-yellow argiope ["are-gee-o-pea"] spiders, *Argiope aurantia*, weave large orb webs in Acadia's meadows in late summer. Once seen, they are never forgotten. Spiders have eight legs, insects have six.

At tide's edge, a **rock crab**, *Cancer irroratus*, lurks in the mud beneath a protective cover of rockweed (lifted by a curious photographer). The shell or carapace of this commercially fished species is pale with reddish flecks.

The **pickerel frog**, *Rana palustris*, is well camouflaged in wet meadows, but this one in a stream flowing into Jordan Pond is as exposed as a standup comedian. Its diet includes insects, spiders, mites, and snails.

Never far from water, this **green frog**, *Rana clamitans*, lures prey in a small pond in the Wild Gardens of Acadia. By staying still, it waits for a beetle, fly, grasshopper, spider, or other unwary tidbit to enter its striking range.

The earliest frog to emerge in spring, the little (body length less than 2.5 inches) **wood frog**, *Rana sylvatica*, is active both day and night in Acadia's cool, moist woods where its diet includes beetles, spiders, earthworms, slugs, and snails.

The **snapping turtle**, *Chelydra serpentina*, has survived for almost 100 million years. When grown, this young one could extend 3 feet head-to-tail. Snappers eat a varied diet including fish, frogs, ducklings, and pickerelweed.

The **painted turtle**, *Chrysemys picta*, is wary and hard to approach, so its colorful beauty often goes unnoticed. It is most often seen at a distance basking in the sun on a log or rock.

The **common garter snake**, *Thamnophis sirtalis*, is indeed common throughout the park. It eats earthworms, insects, leeches, small birds, and rodents. It is eaten in turn by hawks, skunks, foxes, coyotes, raccoons, and larger snakes.

The **common loon**, *Gavia immer*, is a year-round resident of Mount Desert Island, breeding on area ponds, wintering offshore. Poster children of wildness, loons are threatened by heavy-metal from lead sinkers and airborne mercury.

The **red-breasted merganser**, *Mergus serrator*, breeds in Canada, and in winter can often be seen patrolling the shores of Mount Desert Island. Mergansers can get far larger fish down their gullets than their narrow bills would seem to allow.

This **great blue heron**, *Ardea herodias*, displays the webbing between its toes that enables it to stalk worms and fish on mudflats such as those around Thompson Island at low tide. Arriving in April from the southland, herons nest in the area, often on saltwater islands with no terrestrial predators.

This overhead view of a fishhawk or **osprey**, *Pandion haliaetus*, would fill any fish with dread. Ospreys hunt from trees overlooking ponds, or hover, then fold their wings and dive below the surface of fresh or salt water.

Ternlike **laughing gulls**, *Larus atricilla*, are often heard calling as they hunt over salt water, then abruptly dive to glean a tidbit from the surface. Acadia has several other gulls, including Bonaparte's, herring, ring-billed, and great black-backed gulls.

Two immature **bald eagles**, *Haliaeetus leucocephalus*, wait out their adolescence in a typical nest below the crown of a white pine not far from shore. Dark brown their first year, eagles take five years to gain the white head and tail of adult birds.

Soaring **bald eagles** can be told from turkey vultures at a distance by the straight spread of their wings in contrast with the uplifted V on which vultures rock along Acadia's high ridges. Here an adult bald eagle launches into the wind.

The presence of wildlife is often told more in the language of signs than by a personal appearance. Single pellets of **snowshoe hare**, *Lepus americanus*, are common in dense undergrowth throughout the park.

Small clusters of pellets indicate the presence of **white-tailed deer**, *Odocoileus virginianus borealis*. In winter, deer favor the leaves of Northern white cedar, often trimming lower branches as high as they can reach, giving the cedars a pruned look.

The day after a snowstorm is a great time to find out who's where in the park. Tracks of mice, voles, and shrews are common, but sometimes hard to tell apart. This track punctuated by tail drags tells of the galloping journey of a **deer mouse**, *Peromyscus maniculatus*, through the woods.

There is no mistaking tracks of the **porcupine**, *Erethizon dorsatum dorsatum*, which, if the snow is deep enough, are actually two tracks, a wavering one made by the animal's feet, and a wider one brushed out by its quills.

The **beaver**, *Castor canadensis*, is now one of the park's prominent mammals. Once extirpated by heavy trapping, they were reintroduced to the park in the 1920s. Most active at night, beavers are sometimes seen at dawn and dusk.

Acadia has both red and gray squirrels, the first favoring spruce woods, the second oak. This **red squirrel**, *Tamiasciurus hudsonicus*, clamps a spruce cone in its jaws. Red squirrels strip such cones for their seeds.

White in winter, brown in summer, this **snowshoe hare**, *Lepus americanus*, is caught between seasons with a few of its longer white hairs still showing among the shorter brown, its springtime transition a mirror of its grassy habitat.

If any creature can skulk, certainly this **coyote**, *Canis latrans*, is skulking at dawn among icy rocks along a frozen shore. It is likely that the park has five or more breeding pairs of these nocturnal hunters, each with its own territory.

Scats of **red fox**, *Vulpes vulpes*, are often found on rocks along Acadia's hiking trails. When blueberries are ripe, fox scats are often midnight blue, hinting at a varied diet that includes mice, voles, eggs, frogs, worms, insects, and wild berries.

Keen at detecting scents, sounds, and movement, this **white-tailed deer**, *Odocoileus virginianus borealis*, stands briefly before bounding away. Browsers and grazers, deer can be sighted many places in the park at dawn or dusk.

Photographs of Flowers and Fruits

Photographs of Wildlife